SPORTS FOR FUN AND FITNESS

FLAG FOOTBALL FOR FUN AND FITNESS

Dean Smith-Richard

Enslow Publishing
101 W. 23rd Street
Suite 240
New York, NY 10011
USA
enslow.com

Published in 2020 by Enslow Publishing, LLC
101 W. 23rd Street, Suite 240, New York, NY 10011

Library of Congress Cataloging-in-Publication Data

Names: Smith-Richard, Dean author.
Title: Flag football for fun and fitness / Dean Smith-Richard.
Description: New York : Enslow, 2020 | Series: Sports for fun and fitness | Audience: K-4. | Includes bibliographical references and index.
Identifiers: LCCN 2019010921| ISBN 9781978513358 (library bound) | ISBN 9781978513334 (paperback) | ISBN 9781978513341 (6 pack)
Subjects: LCSH: Flag football—Juvenile literature.
Classification: LCC GV952.2 .S55 2020 | DDC 796.332/8—dc23
LC record available at https://lccn.loc.gov/2019010921

Printed in the United States of America

To Our Readers: We have done our best to make sure all website addresses in this book were active and appropriate when we went to press. However, the author and the publisher have no control over and assume no liability for the material available on those websites or on any websites they may link to. Any comments or suggestions can be sent by email to customerservice@enslow.com.

Photo Credits: Flag Football – Research by Bruce Donnola

Cover, p. 1 (football players) RichVintage/E+/Getty Images; cover and interior pages (balls and birdie) Lightspring/Shutterstock.com; p. 7 gurineb/iStock/Getty Images; p. 8 © iStockphoto.com/RichVintage; p. 11 Janet Horton/Alamy Stock Photo; p. 13 dsy88/iStock/Getty Images; p. 14 arek_malang/Shutterstock.com; p. 15 fstop123/iStock/Getty Images; p. 19 Tetra Images, LLC/Alamy Stock Photo; p. 21 © iStockphoto.com/steele2123; p. 22 Zoonar GmbH/Alamy Stock Photo; p. 24 Fran Polito/Moment/Getty Images; p. 25 leisadavis/iStock/Getty Images; p. 26 JoeSAPhotos/Shutterstock.com

Contents

Introduction

Football is a sport played between two teams. Each football team must work together to run plays, score, and—hopefully—win the game. Coaches help plan the game and help players do their very best.

In America, football is played professionally, the largest league being the National Football League (NFL). College teams are also popular, and, in many areas, high school teams are as well. Flag football is a great way to learn the game while avoiding many of the dangers that can come with tackling.

In addition to running, throwing, and catching, flag football can teach you about working with a team and how to make a plan to win! The game changes as you grow up; the field gets bigger and the plays get more complicated.

If you start with flag football, you'll know the game, and be strong enough to play contact football when you're older. If you work hard, practice well, and stay healthy, one day you might even play professional football!

CHAPTER 1

Kick Off!

The game of flag football is a contest between two teams, usually lasting twenty to fifty minutes. Whichever team has the most points when time runs out is the winner.

Timing

Flag football games are divided into halves. The game's length depends on the players' ages. For example, if you are in first grade, you will probably play twenty-minute halves, making the game forty minutes long. Between

Flag football is played on a grass field, with lines often marked in paint or chalk.

the halves is halftime, where players take a break and plan for the second half.

The Field

Field size is another thing that may be different depending on your age or the league. The field is a rectangle,

To win the game, score more touchdowns than the other team—this involves a lot of running!

with **end zones** on each of the short ends. When a team gets to the end zone with the football, they score a **touchdown**.

The long sides of the field are called **sidelines**. If a player crosses a sideline while carrying the ball, the play is over. Each team has its own sideline where coaches and other players stand.

In most flag football leagues, the field is divided in half, with a cone at midfield. Five yards from each end zone is the "no running zone," where the play has to involve a pass instead of a run.

Scoring

Teams score by having a player who is carrying the football run into the end zone or catch a pass in the end zone. This is called a touchdown, and it is worth six points!

After a touchdown, the scoring team has a chance for extra points. They may try for one extra point by running one play from five yards away from the end

SAME GAME, DIFFERENT RULES

Flag football uses a smaller field than tackle football does. Touchdowns in both games are six points. Flag football doesn't have a kicking game so extra points are made by running or throwing rather than by field goals like in tackle football. Extra points can be one or two points, depending on what the coach decides.

zone, or try for two points from ten yards away. If they go for two, the play may be a run or pass.

The Play

Picture your kitchen. Your goal is the cookie jar at the far end, but between you and the goal stands your parents. Your kitchen is the playing field, and you are on **offense**, trying to score a goal (get the cookies). Your parents are playing **defense**—they are defending the goal (the cookies) so you can't reach it.

In flag football, one team is on offense, and they get the ball starting at the five-yard line farthest from their end zone. Everyone on defense stands between the offense and the end zone.

The coach will decide what the play is. A coach will tell each player where to go and what to do. On a passing play, offensive players run in a pattern called a **route**, and the **quarterback** tries to throw the ball to one of them. If it is a running play, the quarterback hands or tosses the ball to another player, who runs toward the end zone.

The play is over when:

- a thrown ball isn't caught and hits the ground, an **incompletion.**
- the ballcarrier has their flag pulled out.
- the ballcarrier steps out of bounds.
- the ballcarrier loses the football, a **fumble.**

The ball is placed where the play ended. The offense then calls another play.

If you don't catch the ball, or drop the ball, the play is incomplete and starts over.

Downs

The offense has four tries, called downs, to get a "first down." A first down is when a player gains ten or more yards. If the offense doesn't make the first down in four tries, the other team gets the ball back.

CHAPTER 2

Teams

On the field, one team plays offense, the other plays defense. The offense has the ball and starts each play. Their goal is to try to score. The defense tries to stop them from scoring.

Flag football usually has six players per team, with five allowed on the field at a time. Tackle football has eleven players from each team on the field at once. For bigger kids, seven-on-seven flag football leagues are also becoming more popular.

Listen to and trust your teammates so everyone can have a great time working toward the same goal.

Positions

The most important thing in football is working together as a team. One player may be very good, but unless everyone works together, plays are unlikely to succeed. It's fun to learn different positions and how to play them. If you do, you can help your team a lot!

The quarterback touches the ball almost every play; it's a position that involves running and throwing.

A lot of the positions you may know from watching tackle football won't be used in flag football. There is no blocking, tackling, or kicking in flag football. It's mostly a running and throwing game. The person who throws the football is called the quarterback. The player who catches the ball is called a **receiver**.

Not Allowed

Everything covered so far has been what *to* do, but there are a few things that aren't allowed in flag football. There is absolutely no tackling or hitting in flag

It's important to listen to your coach in order to stay safe and fit during every game you play.

football. Tackling is dangerous without proper training and **equipment**.

A primary feature of tackle football is blocking, where one player runs into or pushes an opponent to make a

OFFENSE VS. DEFENSE

While other sports, like basketball, hockey, or soccer, have frequent changes of ball possession with the same players playing, this is rare in football. You will play both offense and defense in flag football. You might play one series on offense, then one on defense, and then rest while your teammates take a turn.

path for the ballcarrier. This isn't allowed in flag football, however, for the same reasons as tackling.

Your coach will explain other things that aren't allowed during play, all of which are to make sure you and the other players stay safe.

Health & Safety

Football is an exciting game, but it can be dangerous. No matter how much padding you wear, running full speed into another person may cause **injury**. Coaches can teach you how to play safely. Flag football is a great place to start because it reduces the amount of contact between players. This helps reduce injuries.

Water is your best friend. Your body uses a lot of water playing football, so be sure that you're replacing it. Drink water before and during every practice. Drink water before and during every game. This helps with your energy levels and will keep your muscles from cramping up.

Your coach will probably have you "warm up" your muscles through stretches and light running. Many non-contact injuries can be prevented by having good stretching and warm up habits. Don't rush through them—they are not meant to be done fast.

CHAPTER 3

Skills & Drills

Now that you know how the game works, it's time to see how we actually play it! Offense and defense each have different skills.

Offense

The quarterback touches the ball on nearly every play. The football has laces on one side to help the quarterback get a good grip on the ball before they throw.

Quarterbacks have to be good at throwing, staying mobile, and looking at the entire field. They need to see their teammates, but also the defense. The defense will run at the quarterback, trying to prevent the throw.

Other offensive players will be trying to give the quarterback time to throw, while others will run downfield hoping to catch the pass.

The football has laces to help you get a grip and throw it farther.

The best pass is a tight spiral. That means the ball spins quickly and moves faster toward its target. It takes practice, so don't get discouraged or give up—find someone to play catch with.

If someone is throwing the ball, someone also has to catch it. Receivers run downfield, past the defense, to catch the ball when it is thrown. Get your hands out

THE FORWARD PASS

In the early days of football, every play was a running play. The quarterback had the option to run it or hand it off. Even after throwing the ball first happened, it was rare, and a lot of people thought it wasn't a good way to move the ball. Even teams that passed often completed only short passes, and it was only a few times per game. Now, most college and NFL teams pass the ball more than they run!

early, and make a triangle: put the tips of your thumbs and the tips of your index fingers together with your other fingers spread wide. You want the nose of the ball to go right into that triangle. As soon as it does, pull it toward you.

Defense

In flag football, you will be assigned a player to guard. Your job is to go where they go, stop them from catching the ball if they are a receiver, and pull their flag if they do have the ball. If you're assigned to rush the quarterback, run in and try to grab their flag!

To pull a flag, make sure you have a good grip on it and pull hard! If you can, get in front of the ballcarrier

Learning how to catch a football is as important as throwing, so find someone to play catch with!

In flag football, there's no tackling. You pull a flag off to stop a receiver's progress.

with your legs wide—this makes it hard for them to go around you, and means you can react quickly if they try. Try to get a hand on each side of their waist. Grab the flag as high up as you can, and pull.

CHAPTER 4

Teamwork Makes the Dream Work!

Football is a team sport. Many sports rely on one player being an exceptional athlete to win. Maybe there is a fast runner on your team or someone who throws far. While having a player like that helps, a team that works together will win the day—and have more fun!

You might be a good athlete on your own, but working with a team can make you even better.

How Is a Play Designed?

If you play backyard football, you might tell your friends "just get open," but on a team, plays need to be more organized. If everyone runs to the same spot, or if the quarterback doesn't know where the receivers will be, the play probably won't work.

Most plays for flag football are designed to get one or two receivers open. In the case of a running play, the running back must get "in space," an area where no defenders have an opportunity to stop them.

Get familiar with the football, so you can be comfortable catching it from any position.

In order to get defenders away from where the play is designed to go, receivers will still run like the ball is going to them. A defender still has to guard them. If they don't, and the quarterback sees that, it could result in a big play for the offense!

Once the quarterback throws the ball, the defense swarms toward the ball carrier to try to stop them from scoring.

PLAYING FOOTBALL SAFELY

Football is a contact sport. Flag football is not. While there are many similarities between the games, you should think of flag football as its own sport. Most people who play flag football enjoy watching tackle football and even playing it in leagues with proper equipment. But it is very important to remember the differences. You can injure yourself or someone else by deciding to tackle or block.

What if you are asked to run one of the routes where the ball probably won't come to you? It's still very important to do your best! Every role on the team is important. Your chance to handle the ball will come, and you'll get more opportunities the harder you work.

How Is a Defense Set Up?

There aren't plays for defense in the same way there are for offense. Even though most defensive players will only guard one offensive player, communication and teamwork are still vital.

A running play may have most receivers running straight down the field. Once the ball is out of the quarterback's hands, defensive players have to swarm to the ball and try to pull the ballcarrier's flags. Whoever is rushing the quarterback is usually responsible for calling "run" or "pass" so the rest of the team knows what is happening.

Flag Football Is Fun and Safe

There are flag football leagues across the nation that you can join, all year round! Flag football is a great way to learn teamwork, develop healthy habits, and have a lot of fun!

Words to Know

defense The team that is defending a goal.
end zone The part of the field you reach to score a goal.
equipment Supplies needed to do a job.
fumble Unintentionally dropping the football.
incompletion When a pass is not caught.
injury Harm or damage.
offense The team that is trying to score a goal.
quarterback The offensive player who throws the ball.
receiver The player on offense who catches the ball.
route Designated paths players run down the field.
sideline The long edges of the field.
touchdown A goal for six points.

Learn More

Books

Jacobs, Greg. *The Everything Kids' Football Book, 6th Edition: All-time Greats, Legendary Teams, and Today's Favorite Players—With Tips on Playing Like a Pro.* Avon, MA: Adams Media, 2018.

Laughlin, Kara L. *Flag Football* (Beginning Sports). North Mankato, MN: Child's World Inc., 2016.

Mortensen, Lori. *The End Zone*. Mankato, MN: Stone Arch Books, 2014.

Sports Illustrated Editors. *My First Book of Football: A Rookie Book*. Mankato, MN: Sports Illustrated Kids Rookie Books, 2015.

Websites

American Youth Football and Cheer

www.americanyouthfootball.com

Resources for learning about flag football in your local community.

National Flag Football
www.nationalflagfootball.com
For finding a local league, starting a local league, or attending a tournament, NFF gets you involved.

NFL Flag League Search
nflflag.com/leagueSearch
The National Football League helps kids across the US find flag football leagues in their own neighborhoods.

Index